ENNEAGRAM

Step-by-Step Guide to Self-Discovery and Personal Growth with the 9 Enneagram Personality Types

Lena Lind & Peter Harris

Table of Contents

CHAPTER 1

THE ENNEAGRAM

The Enneagram is a personality typing system based around nine distinct personality types - the theory being that everyone falls into one of these nine categories. Some say that it is an ancient system with its origins traceable to Sufism; others suggest that it is much more recent. However, it is an interesting system with more complexity than meets the eye at first glance.

Our personality develops in childhood - it is our coping strategy which we develop to deal with our own personal environment. There are nine distinctive patterns recognized in the Enneagram, but it also predicts how each of the nine personalities will change under stress and additionally, when we are feeling completely secure.

So, why would we wish to classify anyone as a specific personality type? Well despite the fact that we can go to the moon, most of us have huge difficulty understanding each other. A key to being able to understand other people is to first develop a proper understanding of ourselves and one way of doing that is to take a look at ourself via the Enneagram.

It is not an easy thing to put your own personality under the microscope. You have to be prepared to hear and discover things about yourself that you may not necessarily want to know. You may not like some of the things you discover. There is no point in finding out something about yourself if you are not prepared to address the findings, and changing your behavior takes time, work and a good deal of commitment.

A couple of points to bear in mind when using the Enneagram: firstly, we need to recognize that all personality types are essentially positive and that any negative behavior you may become aware of can be remedied; secondly, you should be very careful about "typing" someone else i.e. putting somebody into a specific Enneagram category.

Knowing where someone else sits on the 9 points can certainly lead to an improved understanding and better communication. But the downside is that it can also lead to stereotyping people and that might lead you to associate specific negative reactions with certain people. For example, we run the risk of deciding that because somebody is a type 7, this means that they are uncommitted and always will be. Or if someone is a type 9, they will be lazy. By stereotyping people and seeking to predict their reactions, we are imposing our own prejudiced ideas and that's just not a good thing.

As we will see, each of the 9 types of personality has positive and negative characteristics. This makes perfect sense, since no human being is perfect, but it is not healthy to concentrate on the negative aspects of anyone's character. Accepting people for who they are and not what we want them to be leads to improved communication and more enjoyable human relationships.

What does the term Enneagram actually mean?

Broken down, the words Ennea and Gram mean "nine" and "model" respectively. So what are the 9 personality types? The actual names will depend on whichever Enneagram teacher you follow but the underlying classifications are broadly the same:

- The Perfectionist/Reformer
- The Giver/Helper
- The Performer/Achiever
- The Tragic Romantic
- The Observer
- The Trooper
- Dreamer/The Epicure
- Confronter/The Boss
- Peacemaker/Mediator

By knowing your own type, you can become much more understanding of other people's reactions. Motivating yourself to achieve things in life will become easier if you understand the drivers for your own behavior.

Followers of the Enneagram believe that everyone has one primary underlying motivational driver that, to a large extent, determines our thoughts, feelings and actions.

This underlying driver or passion creates a person's paradigm or view of life. The passion is given a negative name but it does not mean that the personality type is negative. It means that the personality is primarily addicted to that specific behavior. But this is the raw material - with work, self examination and understanding, all personality types are capable of turning this "negative" into a positive.

For example, type 2, the giver, believes that everyone needs help. The underlying motivation is pride. The type 2 personality takes pride in believing that it can help everyone thus developing an inflated sense of self worth. But by examining and understanding this motivation in life, it can convert this pride to humility and use its natural gift for helping people in a better way.

The underlying driver for type 9 is sloth i.e. being lazy about life. Making decisions takes energy since they must weigh up both sides of the argument, so it is easier just to ignore difficulties and wait for them to go away or for someone else to resolve them. Nines value harmony above everything else. If an understanding of this driver is not developed, they will spend their lives trying to avoid conflict or side stepping arguments.

But Nines, like all the other personality types, can be a fantastic asset to the world. Once they understand that their basic underlying motivation is sloth, they can improve by setting small goals and structuring processes to ensure that they achieve them. Their natural wish to avoid conflict allows them to develop emotional detachment which is very useful in volatile situations.

It is very important to realize that everyone has only one type - you cannot be a member of two camps! Some people, especially those that have just started studying the Enneagram, think that they are a mixture of the different personality types. They identify characteristics which appear to support this theory. Our personal characteristics are not the same as our underlying motivation. We can have similar characteristics and reactions to other people and yet be totally different personality types.

It may be difficult to classify yourself as a particular type. We all have an image of who we are rather than knowledge of who we are. It might be useful to ask a very close friend, whom you trust 100%, to give you some feedback on your personality. Be careful though; not all friendships can survive this type of honesty! And remember that each personality type has positive and negative aspects associated with it. Don't get hung up about the negatives. Instead, pour all your energy into developing the positive aspects of your character.

ENNEAGRAM - THE ABSOLUTE BEGINNER'S GUIDE TO THE ENNEAGRAM OF PERSONALITY

So you are an absolute beginner at the Enneagram... You've heard how amazing and helpful it can be, but you aren't really sure what the big deal is... Well, if you want to get the absolute basics of the Enneagram, then pull up a seat and keep reading.

There are a number of different ways to interpret what we do know about the enneagram. There are a few different "schools of thought" on the subject which you will no-doubt discover more about as you delve deeper into the subject. With that being said, what you are about to read is jaded, opinionated, only partially informed, but hopefully just enough to give you a taste of the Enneagram. And- more important- provides you the push to dig deeper.

The Enneagram, literally, is a symbol. It is a nine-pointed symbol that has shown up in many religions over the last few millennia. Nobody knows for sure how the ancients came up with the study or how they used it until very recently. Enneagram Spectrum sums up the speculations about the origins of the enneagram this way:

"The roots of the Enneagram are disputed. Some authors believe they have found variations of the Enneagram symbol in the sacred geometry of the Pythagoreans who 4000 years ago were interested in the deeper meaning and significance of numbers. This line of mystical mathematics was passed on through Plato, his disciple Plotinus, and subsequent neo-Platonists.

Some believe this tradition found its way into esoteric Judaism through Philo, a Jewish neo-Platonist philosopher, where it later appears as the Tree of Life in the Cabalistic symbolism of ninefoldness.

Variations of this symbol also appear in Islamic Sufi traditions, perhaps arriving there through the Arabian philosopher al-Ghazzali. Around the fourteenth century the Naqshbandi Order of Sufism, variously known as the "Brotherhood of the Bees" (because they collected and stored knowledge) and the "Symbolists" (because they taught through symbols) is said to have preserved and passed on the Enneagram symbol.

Speculation has it the Enneagram found its way into esoteric Christianity through Pseudo-Dionysius (who was influenced by the neo-Platonists) and through the mystic Ramon Lull (who was influenced by his Islamic studies.)

On the frontispiece of a textbook written in the seventeenth century by the Jesuit mathematician and student of arithmology Athanasius Kircher, an Enneagram-like figure appears."

In recent years, the Enneagram was "re-discovered" by Oscar Ichazo, a Chilean philosopher who taught at the Arica Institute in Chile. Ichazo, I believe, was the first person to really apply the laws of the enneagram to the nine laws that operate within the human psyche.

The way the enneagram is understood today is that it is a tool to help understand and articulate nine "filters" that someone can use to see the world. These filters are fluid, intangibles that may or may not exist in reality; however, using them as tools can bring about drastic realizations in relationships or in your personal growth.

THE SPREAD OF ENNEAGRAM AND UNDERSTANDING ITS BASICS

The Enneagram is basically a geometrical figure that the followers of Pythagoras, the great Mathematician have been using for over 2500 years. It's managed to spread across the world thanks to great civilizations such as Babylon and Greece that adopted this system of thought.

It is made up of a total of nine points placed on a circle. Each of these points is clearly defined and labeled using numbers from one to nine. The numbers are used to indicate ones personality, this could be ascertained through Enneagram workshops. However, no personality is higher than the other. So, a person whose personality is found on number one isn't inferior to a person who's found on number nine.

You may wonder what these nine points actually represent; they are personality traits and these are the nine basic traits that contain the personality of every man to walk the Earth. Each of these points is connected to two other points using interconnecting lines, forming a type of star figure.

When you attend Enneagram workshops you will be able to determine which point represents your personality. But, there's nothing great in knowing just that. However, the lines connecting different points are the main catch in this technique. When you're angry you'll move towards a different personality whereas when you're happy you're a whole different person. Therefore, using these lines and the arrows marked on them, one could easily determine the course their minds take when under stress or joy.

Hence, by knowing what one could go through, a coach could help train you to refrain from a bad personality; everyone's got a bad side in them, but it's usually the ugliest part of one's life.

It's not just numbers and lines that make up the Enneagram diagram. In addition to these factors, there are also wings. Wings are placed to refer to the two numbers located near the numbers of your personality type. Most people exhibit the characteristics of one of these wings and very rarely both.

These nine personalities are categorized to fall under three triads namely: Thinking driven personalities, feeling personalities and lastly instinct based personalities. Just think of yourself, you're surely going to fall into one of these categories and hence you'll find a place in the nine as well.

That's all about the structure of the Enneagram, but if you want to check out your personality type, you'll have to find someone who's an expert in it or you could attend Enneagram workshops along with plenty of other participants.

THE ENNEAGRAM STRUCTURE AND DESIGN

The Enneagram is made up of nine points on a circle, each represented by a number from one to nine. The numbers are used to keep things neutral, and a larger digit does not mean a more superior personality type. The nine points represent the nine basic personality types of course, and each type is connected to two others through the interconnecting lines.

The lines show very clearly, the points a person will head towards when feeling good or under stress. In most cases, there will be arrows on the lines indicating the direction towards the integration or growth points, which means the particular personality type we would move towards when we are feeling good or empowered.

Moving in the opposite direction would indicate the particular personality type we would move towards when under stress. This is known as our disintegration or stress points. Moving towards these points does not mean that we will adopt a new personality altogether, it simply means that we will exhibit certain characteristics of that particular personality type. When feeling good, we will show some healthy qualities of our growth point. Conversely, we will also show negative traits of our stress points when under stress.

Then there are also the wings. The wings refer to the two numbers beside each personality type. We will exhibit characteristics of one, or both wings. Though researches have shown that majority of us will have only one dominant wing, it is hard to rule out the possibility of people having two dominant wings, or none at all.

The nine personality types are also divided into different triads based on Instinct, Feeling and Thinking driven personalities. What this means is personality types eight, nine, and one are more instinct driven. They use a lot of their instincts, or referential experience in their behavior. This group also has an issue with aggression, or anger.

Personality types two, three and four are feeling based people. They use a lot of their feelings, and this group has an issue with shame, or the way people look at them. Personality types five, six and seven are the thinking group. So unlike the feeling group, they are more thinking based, and have an issue with fear.

Though there are a few schools of thoughts with the Enneagram, the fundamentals remain constant throughout. In order to use the Enneagram successfully in improving your interpersonal communication skills, it is important to know the basics. This will ensure that the teachings from various sources can serve as add-ons, rather than distractions.

CHAPTER 2

THE ENNEAGRAM PERSONALITY TEST

The Enneagram of Personality is another popular personality test that delves into nine interconnected personality types, focusing on how these types interact with each other.

Compared to the Big Five and the Myers-Briggs tests, the Enneagram is more focused on specific roles of a given personality and its interaction with other personalities.

What is the Enneagram?

Nine personality types mapped on a geometric shape called the enneagram that gave the test its name. The position of the nine types on the enneagram are said to provide insight into their connections with the other types. How a person answers the test's questions determines which number or type they fit into.

The analysis can be likened to that of the Myers-Briggs test in that each personality can be identified with basic strengths and weaknesses that can provide a person with revelations, aiding in their self-understanding and self-awareness.

Beyond the normal personality measures, there is also a level of outside analysis that comes in the form of divergent interpretations, some that eventually tread into mystical and spiritual territory.

What are the nine types?

The nine types are best visualized on the enneagram to understand their relation first:

Each type is represented by a number and name that exemplifies the dominant trait of that personality. Those types are:

- The Reformer: Types that seek improvement, perfection
- The Helper: Types that seek to help, to love and be loved
- The Achiever: Types that seek success, validation
- The Individualist: Types that seek individuality and uniqueness
- The Investigator: Types that seek knowledge, understanding through the observable

- The Loyalist: Types that seek firm beliefs, trust

- The Enthusiast: Types that seek satisfaction, pleasure

- The Challenger: Types that seek self-sufficiency, control

- The Peacemaker: Types that seek harmony, wholeness

Depending on which type you have, you might also have what's known as a 'wing'-- which is simply traits from one of the two personality types adjacent to yours on the enneagram. So a type 9 might have a type 1 or type 8 wing.

The lines that connect the personalities are interpreted in a few ways, ranging from one personality's connection to other connecting types, to how a personality can adapt and change into other personality types in stressful or relaxing situations.

Criticism of the Enneagram test

More so than even the Myers-Briggs test, the Enneagram has been widely criticized of employing pseudoscience -- meaning it has little actual scientific backing or merit to point to.

Some disagree with that harsh assessment, saying even though there's little rigor in the way of peer-reviewed studies on the test, it still functions as a valuable tool for self-insight.

The largest piece of criticism about the Enneagram model is that the nine types are largely ambiguous to the point that it's easy to shoehorn someone into any one of the nine types based off their answers -- likening it to the "Barnum Effect" associated with fortunetelling and astrology.

AN EXAMPLE OF ENNEAGRAM TEST

This Enneagram test it has 171 items and it will take you about 20 minutes to complete. The accuracy of the final version of the test is rather high, considering the data so far. The sample consisted of 198 people that had previously decided on their Enneagram type (of course, all 9 Enneatypes were represented in the sample).

The highest score indicated the correct type in 82, 6% of the cases. The main type was among the first two highest scores in 95, 6% of the cases, and among the first three in 97, 2% of the cases.

PART I: SELECTION

Check all the traits that you think apply to you:

- Pragmatic
- Aesthetic
- Detached
- Clumsy
- Spontaneous
- Powerful
- Indulgent
- Nit-picking
- Sentimental

- Self-promoting

- Capricious

- Reserved

- Alert

- Joker

- Vigorous

- Patient

- Principled

- Demonstrative

- Go-getter

- Dramatic

- Receptive

- Ingenious

- Rigorous

- Warmhearted

- Exuberant

- Reactive

- Vindictive

- Arrogant

- Isolated

- Adventurous

- Combative

- Stubborn

- Manipulative

- Conscientious
- Romantic
- Restless
- Emotional
- Serious
- Empathetic
- Abstract
- Joyful
- Procrastinating
- Questioning
- Adaptable
- Perfectionist
- Sensitive
- Loyal
- Correct
- Image oriented
- Childlike
- Relaxed
- Insightful
- Intimidating
- Selfless
- Domineering
- Organized
- Valuable

- Trustworthy
- Versatile
- Easy-going
- Worrier
- Tough
- Investigative
- Moody
- Self-righteous
- Giving
- Ambitious
- Imprudent
- Intense
- Misunderstood
- Self-sacrificing
- Cerebral
- Trusting
- High-strung
- Instinctual
- Efficient
- Clingy
- Nostalgic
- Scattered
- Secretive
- Content

- Blunt

- Critical

- Vain

- Refined

- Passive

- Ambivalent

- Willful

- Playful

- Helpful

PART II: SCALING

On a scale from 1 to 5, grade these statements according to how much they characterize you and the way you behave in general.

1. I am a cheerful, enthusiastic person with lots of plans and things to do: I love having fun, trying new things and living life to the full. I'm versatile and epicurean.

2. Although I am a selfless and generous person, I can't help feeling disappointed when I receive no appreciation for the support I give.

3. I consider myself different from most people and many times I feel envious of their normality and simple happiness. I feel something is always missing from my life and I long for it.

4. I'm open-minded and receptive to many ideas and viewpoints, but sometimes I have trouble deciding where I stand on an issue. I am usually flexible but somewhat indecisive.

5. I'm a highly-motivated achiever and I know how to adapt myself and my behavior to people and circumstances in order to succeed.

6. I have a clear set of standards and principles that I follow and I want others to respect them as much as I do. I can be rather conservative in this respect.

7. I have a strong need to acquire knowledge and information about the subjects that interest me – I can isolate myself for hours and days in a row to study and learn.

8. My temper is explosive and I often have outbursts of rage although they don't typically last long - I'm impulsive, aggressive and not afraid of open conflict.

9. I can be a faultlessly loyal friend, partner and employee – honest, devoted and reliable. I could forgive anything but betrayal, which makes me lose my trust for good.

10. I can easily put my feelings aside when I need to – I'm not very in touch with my emotions and I tend to ignore them when they get in the way to my goals.

11. I am a curious person with a very active mind - I have loads of ingenious ideas and interests in a wide range of domains, although I don't get to deepen many of them.

12. I am organized, punctual and methodical and I feel many things depend on me to solve them – I usually take responsibility to straighten things out without being asked to.

13. My emotions are real and important to me, they define who I am and I like to cultivate and express them in unique and unexpected ways.

14. I can be quite distrustful of people and skeptical of unproven beliefs – I'm great at reading between the lines, debunking faulty theories and scoping out hidden motivations.

15. I'm bothered by feelings and emotions so I detach myself from them – this is why I usually appear cold and overly cerebral to others.

16. I'm rather laid-back, easy-going and not very ambitious – I believe things will sort out by themselves. As a consequence I'm sometimes forgetful, procrastinating and unconcerned.

17. I enjoy helping others and assisting them with their personal problems – I give other people a lot of my time and energy. Being needed makes me feel loved.

18. I believe nothing is impossible, therefore I tend to push myself and others to the limit. I want to leave a mark, do something that will have a real impact in the world.

19. I'm often hurt by criticism or harsh remarks and tend to withdraw and sulk about them by myself. It's easy for me to feel rejected or abandoned because I'm very sensitive.

20. It can be hard for me to finish the things I start. I become enthused with new possibilities and tend to forget about following through with my previous commitments.

21. I can be very hard on myself when I make a mistake – I strive for perfection and I get angry at myself when I can't reach it. I do the same with other people too.

22. My mind is focused and intense and I can be very perceptive and insightful – I become an expert in the fields that I study and trust my intelligence more than anything else.

23. I am strong, direct and fearless – I like taking risks and ending up victorious. Failure doesn't scare me; it only makes me more determined.

24. I tend to openly show my feelings towards others, either verbally or physically (by touching, hugging) – I come across as sentimental and empathetic.

25. I am a rather anxious and nervous person, who tends to worry about a lot of things that might go wrong – from health to finances. I can appear quite fidgety at times.

26. My image is very important to me so I am really talented at making a good impression on people and dressing for success on any occasion.

27. People tend to feel comfortable around me, because I'm tolerant, unpretentious and dislike conflict. I'm a good mediator because I see all sides of an issue.

28. I see most things in terms of moral right and wrong and I won't compromise what I believe is right – I consider myself an upright idealist.

29. I value my freedom most of all and I need to have as many options available as possible – I have problems with long-term commitments and being stuck in things.

30. People's company can feel draining and invasive after a relatively short while so I tend to isolate myself and avoid too much social contact – I value my privacy.

31. Although I'm generally cooperative and open to suggestions, I can sometimes get very stubborn about some things –immutable and resolute in the face of opposition.

32. Although I value my independence, I have some people that I trust and admire enormously and whom I'd follow anywhere. When I'm in, I'm in all the way.

33. Leadership comes naturally to me – I'm tough, enterprising and pragmatic and know how to get others to do as I say. I can be quite bossy and intimidating.

34. I tend to have special and melancholic moods which I enhance through imagination – I lose myself in romantic fantasies and imagine things and conversations that did not happen.

35. I'm attracted to rescuing and supporting hurt and troubled individuals, sometimes to the point of neglecting my own needs and even health, on the long term.

36. I am very ambitious and tend to be a bit of a workaholic – free time is sometimes awkward to me because I feel aimless and unproductive.

37. I can be judgmental and critical of others and tend to consider most people as chaotic and irresponsible, so I might come across as patronizing, rigid or controlling.

38. I'm very proud of myself and my accomplishments, so at times I do tend to brag about them a bit and act precious. I suppose I can appear somewhat narcissistic.

39. I tend to ask myself a lot of questions and second-guess my decisions, which can make me appear somewhat ambivalent and contradictory.

40. I abhor looking weak or vulnerable, so I make sure I'm as independent and powerful as possible. I sometimes take other people under my protection to prove my strength.

41. I tend to maintain a neutral approach to life – I am somewhat disconnected from my feelings and wishes. I can appear a bit indifferent, absent but also calm in a crisis.

42. I am deeply introspective and fully dedicated to discovering who I really am. I am not afraid of my dark side or my most disturbing emotions.

43. Boredom is one the worst things that can happen to me so I avoid being alone for too long. I need lots of friends, adventure and variety.

44. I'm a considerate and nurturing friend, although I sometimes do tend to become a little manipulative and meddling. I think I know what's best for others.

45. I'm very curious and like to investigate and study things in depth. I draw my own conclusions after careful consideration and tend to disregard common knowledge and other's opinions.

PART III: DISTINCTION

From each of the pairs below, choose the trait that best describes you. If it is hard to pick, go with your first instinct.

- Efficient, disciplined introspective, bohemian
- Autonomous, impartial subjective, partisan
- Amusing, outspoken successful, diplomatic
- Flattering, effusive frank, unpretentious
- Organized, mature spontaneous, childlike
- Strong, down-to-earth sensitive, idealistic
- Sharp, observant relaxed, unfocused
- Logical, criticizing loving, complimentary
- Awkward, transparent smooth, chameleonic
- Proud, obliging moderate, standoffish
- Shy, melancholic fun loving, assertive
- Aggressive, impulsive reclusive, analytical
- Worrying, unsure carefree, confident
- Involved, rule-bound detached, iconoclastic

- Mysterious, individualistic friendly, altruistic

- Strange, solitary admirable, competitive

- Self-certain, composed self-questioning, reactive

- Intimate, codependent flighty, adventurous

- Direct, forceful reserved, tactful

- Vulnerable, self-revealing restrained, self-protective

- Nervous, hesitant powerful, resolute

- Hyperactive, stimulating patient, peaceful

- Firm, principled adaptable, pragmatic

- Engaging, sociable quiet, reclusive

- Attractive, well-mannered domineering, defiant

- Tolerant, indifferent demanding, controlling

- Tough, intimidating empathetic, dramatic

- Easy-going, agreeable driven, arrogant

- Refined, delicate witty, realistic

- Playful, liberal hard-working, bossy

- Whimsical, emotional controlled, disciplined

- Cool, egocentric selfless, sentimental

- Temperamental, complex calm, uncomplicated

- Focused, withdrawn scattered, outgoing

- Passionate, excitable unconcerned, nonchalant

- Abrupt, combative formal, ethical

Before you're done...

Do you already know your Enneagram Type?

CHAPTER 3

SUBTYPES IN THE ENNEAGRAM: WHY THEY MATTER

Types form the foundation of enneagram trance but there are a number of other factors that help to articulate individuals within types. One of these categories is that of "sub-types". Subtypes are lie proverbial three legged stools. Usually there will be one leg that is the strongest in a person's ego state, followed by a second subtype that the person also embraces to a lesser degree. The third leg will be missing for most people. This missing piece is largely the cause of imbalance within the ego state. Consider these three subtypes:

- Self-preservation- These people are typically concerned primarily with their own safety and that of those around them. They are the people who are stocking up for Y2K and keeping back stocks of basic supplies both in their cars and in their homes. Preparation, regardless of their basic type, is a hallmark of these subtypes.

- Sexual or One to one-- These people prefers one to one contacts and conversations and interactions. While they can function in social groups, they will tend to seek out individuals within groups for much of their connection. Their preference gives them an intensity that sets them apart from the other two subtypes.

- Herd Instinct -- These people are joiners. They get their identity largely from what they associate with. They are the people who love sports teams, political parties, brand name clothing and other associations with others. Being an individual is not as important to them as their affiliations with group identities and following the crowd.

Subtypes are extremely useful in understanding our own preferences in social interaction and the particular intensity that we bring to situations. When we're working to understand our own types or those of people around us, it's vitally important to consider subtypes, both the primary and the secondary types, as well as the third one that is being rejected as unimportant. For example, someone who has little or no herd instinct will appear highly individualistic and likely have trouble bonding in identity in groups or networking with groups. This can be a handicap in professional/career development in some professions. Those who have trouble in one to one interactions will find it more difficult to interview, to sustain intimate relations with one to one subtype people and sometimes can appear to lack certain depth in conversational skills. Those who lack self preservation may have trouble understanding when danger or the need for self protection is truly present, retaining little or nothing that they might need for their very real safety.

The enneagram is not a simple '9 types fit all' system. There are a number of elements that go into understanding trance. Subtypes are all part of the subtle color variations that we see in the nine types and need to be considered as we look at ourselves and others in their daily functioning.

THE ENNEAGRAM PERSONALITY TYPES

The Perfectionist

These are people with a need to get things right. Perfectionists are usually critical, idealistic, and judgmental. Decisions are made with an internalized 'single correct way' in mind. Their work is meant to reflect extremely high standards set by themselves. Continually, they are teaching, preaching, and monitoring others. This causes others to feel nit-picked or rejected. Perfectionist fiercest anger is directed toward themselves. At their best, Perfectionists are honest, idealistic, visionaries. They have a clear vision of what should be, with the ability to direct others.

The Helper

Helpers strive to be appreciated. They give with the intention of reciprocal gratitude. Helpers are relationship oriented with an emotionally seductive attitude. Sweet and manipulative, helpers make themselves indispensable to and adored by others. This is their path to influence and seek power. Helpers have impeccable radar for others feeling, preferences, and appetites. They excel in customer services, are genuinely sensitive, and humble. Helpers serve and bring out the best in others.

The Producer

Producers are more than likely workaholics. They enjoy being applauded for getting the job done. Producers can be high performing, enthusiastic, and competitive. It is essential that they be rewarded for their achievements. Some might say that Producers are self involved and obsessed with image. They come off as insensitive, superficial, artificial and expedient. Producers are often seen merely as their resume. At their best Producers are eager, efficient leaders with the ability to problem solve and influence others.

The Connoisseur

It is easy for a Connoisseur to gravitate toward the beautiful, authentic, true and unusual. These people are romantic and melancholic. Connoisseurs manifest impeccable taste within their concerns. They look for deeper meaning underneath the surface. Feelings are what drive their decisions. Connoisseurs seem to be satisfied with the impeccable. They can seem intense or snooty. At their best they are creative and imaginable. Connoisseurs love the attractiveness, taste, and elegance in the world.

The Sage

Sages seek mastery over their personal domains. They are emotionally detached. It is said that sages observe the world from safe vantage points. Here they can stockpile facts, theories, and information. Sages do not rely on relationships but instead camouflage themselves and minimize needs. Others see them as emotionally detached, as they hide behind whatever they can find. At best, Sages are sensitive, brilliant, respectful, intense, entrepreneurs. Committed and most wizards in their fields.

The Troubleshooter

Paranoid at best, troubleshooters are preoccupied with worse case scenarios. Trust is a huge issue. They are over prepared and obsessed with what could possibly go wrong. Others may find their procrastination frustrating. Troubleshooters can be faithful, imaginative, original thinkers, intuitive, committed, sensitive, and courageous. They are known for defending their team, their boss, and themselves. Troubleshooters are terrific at pointing out pitfalls and hidden motives along the way.

The Visionary

Visionaries stay positive and keep all options open. They engage, plan, and have high energy romances. Visionaries have difficulty growing up. They are known as superficial Peter Pans. It is not easy for visionaries to consider pitfalls. Therefore, they avoid completion, pain, conflict, ordinary commitments, and routine work. Although they initiate progress they often times neglect to follow through. The best Visionaries are gifted, witty, inspirational, and charming. Their ideas and enthusiasm pull people toward them.

The Top Dog

Power and control are what Top Dogs seek. They express their feelings freely and loudly. Top Dogs are described to be domineering and blunt. They loudly seek out confrontations believing the truth often comes out in a fight. They focus on their own powers and others shortcomings. Others may be repelled by their flamboyant bullying. At best Top Dogs are nurturing of the underdogs with whom they are in charge of.

The Mediator

Mediators seek to include all people and all points of view. These people compromise easily. They can see the feelings, needs, and enthusiasms of others. Others may see Mediators as neglectful or spacey. At their best, mediators lead by inspiring others. They are warm and openhearted individuals. Mediators are naturally in touch with the flow of the group. Therefore, mediators are excellent diplomats, team builders, and boundary spanners.

ENNEAGRAM TYPE 1 - THE PERFECTIONIST

This personality type is also called the Reformer. Their underlying motivation is anger. They pursue perfection in life and when it doesn't happen, they often get angry and then very anxious. They are extremely loyal people with high moral values who work very hard to protect and look after their family and loved ones.

They have many positive qualities. They have an excellent eye for detail for example. In effect, they will do all the letters 'I' and cross all the letters 'T' in everything they do. Driven by a harsh inner critic, they always try very hard to make sure everything they do is as perfect as it can be. This triggers their need to improve, which can be beneficial for all concerned, but which can also prove to be burdensome to both the type 1 and those who are on the receiving end of the type 1's reform efforts.

But they also have negative qualities. They can be very quick to judge other people although they feel very guilty doing so. Despite their obvious gifts, they often cannot appreciate their own value and tend to struggle with their inner critic - the voice inside their head telling them how useless they are. They tend to believe that others are just being nice when they give them a complement.

As they are perfectionists, they put themselves under constant pressure to do better, work harder and achieve more. This can make them appear pushy and uncaring in group situations.

Are you a Perfectionist?

- Do you have a loud inner voice continually criticizing you?

- Do you often wonder how you could have done something better or faster?

- Do you have difficulty accepting compliments about your work?

- Do you wish you were easier going?

- Do you redo the work of others as it doesn't live up to your standards?

- Have other people called you a perfectionist?

If you have identified yourself as a perfectionist then try these simple tips to help restore the positive aspects of your personality type:

- Learn how to accept a compliment and believe in its sincerity
- Learn how to relax more
- You need to take some personal time out to just enjoy yourself
- Find ways of silencing your inner critic
- Retrain your thoughts to become more positive

Work on the most negative qualities of your personality type: a tendency to get angry with others, an inclination to be judgmental and a belief that it is your role to set the world straight regardless of the consequences.

Following study and evaluation of yourself, you can learn to manage these negatives so that your personality will attach itself to the positive characteristics of your type. Being hard working, direct when appropriate and attempting to change the world for the benefit of others are your positive qualities and these will be naturally highlighted when you learn to control the negatives.

ENNEAGRAM TYPE 2 - THE GIVER/HELPER

Helpers want to help the world and its mother. They tend to take on everyone's problems as they believe that they can fix them. Their primary motivation is pride - everyone, they tend to think, needs help.

Their positive qualities are that they are extremely kind and helpful to their fellow beings. They make wonderful supporters and right-hand people as they essentially enjoy being the providers of help. The welfare of the individual is the most important thing.

The giver personality type does not, by and large, tend to make a good leader. They generally do not like goals and are not primarily task orientated. They can allow themselves to become too emotionally involved which can often lead to negative feelings, such as the impression of being used. These negative feelings can sometimes cause a lack of objectivity and they can easily lose sight of their role.

Helpers are usually spared from having to deal with their own neediness and problems as they are far too busy helping others. They can often be poor decision makers as they often miss the big picture - the needs of the individual they are helping at that moment in time are paramount as far as they are concerned.

Are you a helper?

- Do you hate doing certain tasks you have to perform because you just don't see the point in them?

- Are you happiest when you are helping others achieve their goals or sort out their problems?

- Do you often feel taken for granted as people that you have helped fail to thank you enough?

- Do you find that you often start projects but fail to see them through as you are distracted by other people and their issues?

If you have identified yourself as a helper then try these simple tips to help restore the positive aspects of your personality type:

- Identify your own needs and spend some time on meeting these needs. Make a diary note if necessary, perhaps telling yourself that you cannot help x, y or z until you have done at least one thing on your list to help yourself.

- Start believing that you are not responsible for everyone else and you cannot fix all the problems.

- Get better at identifying when people really need your help and when they are best left alone to sort themselves out.

You can turn your tendency to seek approval from others and your tendency to crave attention into the more positive attributes of compassion and focus on other human beings. This will help you to build long lasting friendships that help meet your underlying motivation to feel needed in a much more positive way.

ENNEAGRAM TYPE 3 - THE PERFORMER

Performers are free thinkers who tend to harbor a deep-seated fear of failure. They often measure success based upon the respect and approval they receive from others. They are image orientated people who can provide an outwardly positive, well groomed appearance despite sometimes feeling completely desperate and negative about their lives. They are great politicians as they instinctively know when to say nothing. They also excel in selling and advertising roles as their positivity and go getting approach tends to attract other people.

Their positive qualities can make them great leaders, but in their drive for success they can sometimes cause resentment and frustration. They will rely on their natural charisma and charm to get them out of these sticky personal relationship difficulties. They are natural talkers and being so optimistic and confident, they believe they could probably sell snow to the Eskimos.

The negative side of their personality type is that they cannot bear any criticism, even if meant constructively. They often interpret being criticized as failing. Being masters of communication, they can easily use sarcasm as a means of putting someone else down. As their primary motivator is a fear of failure, they will be intolerant of any behavior which is socially unacceptable. This can extend to their children's poor table manners, rudeness or boldness. Anything that could potentially reflect badly on them is simply not tolerated.

Are you a performer?

- Do you often feel like you are wearing a mask or acting a role? The world sees a confident, go getter whilst you might see someone who is a bit of a failure?

- Do you have very few close friends but a number of friendly acquaintances mainly related to your field of work?

- Is it difficult for you to relax and just do nothing?

- Do you worry about letting people get too close to you in case they see you are in fact a "failure"?

- Do you worry that other people you work with will eventually find out that you are not really capable of doing anything right?

Try these simple tips to help restore the positive aspects of your personality type if you are a succeeder:

- Allow other people to love the real you not your job or your financial status

- Learn to accept yourself - get rid of the mask. Whilst nobody likes a serial moaner, people who are always on top of the world can be difficult to live with too

- Try to appreciate your life as it currently stands. Stop waiting for the next pay rise or promotion to enjoy life.

- You can learn to channel your negative characteristic of frantic activity into goal setting. Instead of focusing on outer success, use your natural abilities to work for the benefit of everyone's success.

ENNEAGRAM TYPE 4 - THE TRAGIC ROMANTIC

Types 4 tend to see their lives as a kind of tragedy. They tend to be constantly living in the past and feeling that life has somehow passed them by. They fundamentally feel that something is missing as they cannot seem to accept the ordinariness of their everyday lives. However, they do tend to like being the centre of attention.

The Romantic - in the sense of the romantic movement in art (wild, Byronic) is also known as the Individualist; they have clear values and standards and tend to be very sensitive. When this sensitivity is used positively, they are sensible, perceptive people aware of the needs and wants of their fellow human beings. They make very loyal friends and show great compassion for other people. They make great teachers as they have the ability to inspire others, even to greatness.

But when used negatively, this sensitivity translates into highly strung, touchy people who can be very difficult to live with. They can be quick to delegate responsibility for everything including their own lives as they get easily bored with "normal" things. They want the "romantic dream" but often lose interest when it actually becomes available.

Past relationships become more "perfect" as time passes and the current relationships pale in comparison. They cannot see that their current life would make them happy if they just accepted what they had.

Some questions to ask if you think you may be a four:

- Are you locked in the past examining relationships that might have been?

- Do you tend to gravitate towards the dramatic side of life - clothes, food, and people?

- Do you often experience so many different emotions that you are not sure what you are feeling and become overwhelmed?

- Do you suffer a sense of loss or abandonment even when in a close nurturing relationship?

Tips to try to minimize the negative aspects include:

- Mourn a past relationship but make sure you can let it go. Stop dwelling on and reinventing the past.

- Work on reducing the dramatic tantrums and learn how to control your mood swings.

- Recognize the merits of your current life and partner.

- Use your sensitivity to help others deal with their pain whilst building a support network to comfort you when you need it.

You can minimize your introspective behavior and feelings of discouragement and concentrate on loving yourself and using your natural abilities to show compassion and help your fellow man.

ENNEAGRAM TYPE 5 - THE OBSERVER

As the name suggests, this personality type watches the world go by from the safety of their ivory tower. They aim to achieve greater clarity and understanding of the world around them. They don't like confrontation or dissent so tend to take the third party view, refusing to get involved in any family squabbles.

They tend to make headstrong leaders as they are fully confident in their own abilities. They "know" that they will either have a deeper understanding of the subject matter already or else have the ability to learn it. Observers are happy to make decisions in the workplace as they believe in logical thinking but will pass the responsibility for emotional decisions i.e. those involved in a relationship to the other party.

The positive aspects of this personality type are their curiosity in people and the world around them, and this makes them willing to try new ideas. They have great courage and tend to be non judgmental of other human beings. They encourage others to develop their own independence as they are happy to delegate and trust others in their team.

The negative behavior with this personality type is, as with the other types, a distortion of their strengths. As they are analytical by nature, they believe that everyone is in control of their life so can be quite unsympathetic. They do not believe in fate so any misfortune you may suffer is down to your own incompetence.

Observers tend to be very bad at asking for help as they believe that they already know everything they need to know or have the ability to find out. This makes them very resourceful people but they can also be difficult for others to live with.

Are you an observer? Try these questions:

- Do you have a thirst for knowledge and information?
- Do you find other people's lack of logical thinking to be extremely irritating?
- Do you find yourself becoming excited by anything new, unexpected and are quickly bored by repetition?

Some simple tips to help reinforce the positive side of this personality type:

- Learn to value spontaneity - not everything has to be planned down to the last detail.
- Believe in your freedom to express your emotions.
- It is OK to ask for help - you cannot possibly know everything.
- Instead of being selfish and uncompromising, acknowledge the world around you and use your knowledge freely to help others.

ENNEAGRAM TYPE 6 - THE TROOPER/GUARDIAN

The Trooper is also known as the Guardian by some teachers involved in the Enneagram. This personality type is always seeking to avoid danger. Their underlying motivation is a deep rooted lack of self confidence so they seek out groups with well defined values.

The positive side of this personality type is that they make fantastic friends and companions. They are loyal, courageous and totally dedicated to their group of friends. They genuinely care for others and work to make the world a better place for everyone to enjoy. Warmth and affection come naturally as does a good sense of humor. They value status and work very hard to attain it.

Acutely aware of where the danger is in the environment, there are both phobic and counter-phobic sixes. Phobic sixes tend to avoid danger whereas counter-phobic sixes are aware of danger but also prepared to deal with it head on. A high number of counter-phobic sixes are to be found in what might be considered dangerous occupations.

As this personality type lacks self confidence, they can have a blinding faith in authority. They will follow the authority figure regardless, adopting a position of "they will know best". When asked to make spontaneous contributions to decision making, they are often indecisive and speak haltingly as they question what they are saying. They are often apprehensive, insecure and anxious and need to feel that they fit with their group.

Do you fit this personality type? Try these questions:

- Do you love entertaining people in the comfort of your home?

- Do you prefer to have a day full of activities and hate having free time as you are not sure how to spend it?

- Do you find it difficult to make decisions, preferring others to do it for you?

- Do you prefer an authoritarian boss who lays out very strict rules for you to follow rather than a more laid back boss who likes delegating responsibility and decision making to you?

If you fit into this personality type, try these tips:

- Avoid procrastination by setting yourself deadlines for achievement of specific goals.

- Don't avoid a task just because the instructions are confusing - instead, ask for clarification.

- Seek feedback from a group of trusted friends and family so that you can deal with your self confidence issues.

- Having a strong conscience and being faithful to others is preferable to being helpless and unsure of yourself.

ENNEAGRAM TYPE 7 - THE DREAMER/EPICURE

Types 7 tend to believe that the world is full of opportunities and so they spend all their time and energy searching for ways to make life easier. They are highly intuitive people with high energy levels and they find it difficult to relax as they are so absorbed fitting together the pieces of life's puzzle.

Their underlying motivation is a fear of discomfort or pain and they go to great lengths to avoid experiencing these feelings. They are compulsive optimists. There is a solution to every problem - you just have to find it.

From a positive perspective, Types 7 are often visionaries and idealists who may have the means to solve our global problems. They believe that everyone is good at heart even if it takes a machine to dig deep enough to find it. By trusting in their fellow man, they tend to bring out the best in people. They make ideal entrepreneurs as they don't believe in failure and will change tack at a moment's notice if that is required.

But Dreamers often find it difficult to see a project through to the end because they are so focused on having fun and gritting your teeth and grinding out a result is often not much fun. The more successful ones generally employ another personality type to undertake such tasks as they acknowledge their weakness. Dreamers crave pleasure which they get by pursuing new challenges. This personality type has been linked to the "deadly" sin of gluttony as they will feed their addiction to pleasure above and beyond almost everything else.

So do you fit the Dreamer role?

- Do you immediately start looking for solutions when you are presented with a problem even if it belongs to someone else?
- Can you talk to anyone? Do people seek you out at dinner parties and other social occasions? Were you the most popular kid in school?
- Do people often comment on how "gifted" you are?

Tips for dealing with the negative side of the dreamer type:

- Make it a specific goal to follow through one task from beginning to the end.
- Recognize that having multiple projects on the go at one time can be a way of trying to escape from reality.
- Stop thinking that anyone who disagrees with you is criticizing you. Constructive criticism is often useful.

- If you find yourself acting eccentrically or living in fantasy, embrace your real life and find reasons to be optimistic and radiate good cheer in life.

ENNEAGRAM TYPE 8 - THE CONFRONTER/BOSS

Big on authenticity - they tend to call a spade a spade- and perhaps, as a consequence, somewhat low on empathy, types 8 tend to thrive on challenge and are prepared to deal with just about anything that life has to offer. They see themselves as the "knights" of the kingdom and their job is to protect the innocent and the less able.

Their underlying motivation is a feeling of weakness so to avoid this; types 8 develop a heightened sense of power. You can feel their presence as soon as they enter a room. These personality types thrive in the military or political world. From a positive viewpoint, their personality make up means that they are extremely resourceful and will always stand up for those they view to be less able. They also encourage others to have more belief in themselves and to stand firm in their convictions.

They tend to believe that the end justifies the means so manipulate situations to their advantage. They tend to see situations in a black and white way which can cause them to be inflexible. Their underlying desire is for power, not prestige, which can lead to bullying. They have the innate ability to spot a weakness in their opponents. They may not always win the battle, but if you take them on, you will know you have been in a fight.

Do you think you may fit the role of the Confronter/Boss?

- Do you often find yourself fighting for other people's rights with no fear of any repercussions?
- Do people who take ages to make a point irritate you the most?
- Are you a natural leader?
- Do you think you are a practical person i.e. the one to get the job done?

Some tips to help make the positive side of your personality type shine through:

- Learn to control your "confrontational" side.
- Life is not black and white. Human beings create complex problems and it may not always be apparent which side is the "right" one.
- Learn to allow others to take the lead sometimes.

- Learn to manage your anger properly. Suppressing your angry feelings isn't enough as that can cause problems too.

- Work on your tendency to bully and be controlling. Concentrate on remembering that everyone is not created equal - some are not as strong as others and it is these people that need your protection not you're bullying.

ENNEAGRAM TYPE 9 - MEDIATOR/PEACEMAKER

This personality type wants to create harmony between themselves and the rest of the world. They will suppress their emotions for fear of rocking the boat. They believe that you shouldn't make waves - you can't please everyone so why bother even trying. Their underlying motivation is laziness. They can be resourceful and tend to apply common sense to resolve any problems or issues they come across. You have probably heard someone being described as a "gentle giant" - this would be a perfect description for this personality type.

Once they have mastered their personality type, the positive elements of inner peace and tranquility make them experts at dealing with difficult people. Being even tempered, they do not rise to the bait and hence their presence has a calming influence on most volatile situations.

They are able to maintain a healthy detachment thus preventing the need to take sides in an argument. For this reason they make excellent arbiters.

But mediators can suffer from a lack of self esteem which causes them to dwell on the past. They don't value themselves or their input to relationships which helps them to justify their underlying motivation of laziness. Their view being: my input isn't that important so why waste my time and energy putting it across.

In the working world, although very capable at their jobs, they will often avoid getting promoted into positions that involve stress and responsibility. As they wish to avoid conflict at all costs, they will often ignore even a direct question if they know that the answer will upset anyone. They will maintain this silence until the other party either solves the problem or gives up trying. By enforcing silence, they don't have to cause conflict or deal with the fallout.

So are you a mediator?

- Do people comment on the fact that you will do anything to avoid an argument, even leaving if necessary?
- Do you work on the basis that if you keep your thoughts to yourself, you can't cause an argument?
- Do people perceive you as easy going whilst inside you may be in turmoil?

- Do you prefer the simple pleasures in life?

Some tips to help your positive qualities shine through:

- Try setting some personal goals and impose deadlines by which they must be achieved.

- Learn to recognize what you want rather than what others want.

- Using small steps, try making a point of making a decision.

- When someone asks you a question, think about what you want and admit to it rather than keeping quiet.

- Stop doubting yourself and learn to accept and love yourself. You have the ability to move mountains once you maximize the positive aspects of your personality.

CHAPTER 4

ENHANCING RELATIONSHIPS WITH THE ENNEAGRAM

What difference would it make to your life if your relationships, at home and at work, were based on mutual understanding and respect, where you inspire each other to be your best and enjoy the differences between you? The Enneagram is a powerful and still surprisingly little known approach to understanding our personality type and that of the people we are close to, and it helps us to create and enjoy wonderfully fulfilling, happy relationships that just get better over time.

With insights from the Enneagram, we can maximize the potential for fun, connections, love, and growth in our relationships, rather than endure problems based on misunderstandings.

How does it work then, I can hear you asking? Well, first you need to understand what type you are and identify what areas of development you have within your type---and by the way, it's much easier to work on your development when you have specific, individual areas to look at, rather than a generic, one size fits all self-help approach.

What is Your Enneagram Type?

There are 9 basic personality types, each of which has one of three essential frameworks through which they view and filter the world: analytic, where we have an intellectual first response; emotional, where our first response is a feeling one; and instinctive, where we first have a gut reaction to a situation. Just knowing which of these 3 frameworks is primary, immediately gives us a short-cut to deeper understanding.

Type 1: The Reformer, idealistic and perfectionist

Type 2: The Helper, motivated by the need to be valued

Type 3: The Achiever, ambitious and driven

Type 4: The Individualist, romantic and artistic

Type 5: The Thinker, analytical and detached

Type 6: The Loyalist, motivated by the need for security

Type 7: The Adventurer, enthusiastic and fun-loving

Type 8: The Challenger, assertive and direct

Type 9: The Peacemaker, mediating and non-confrontational

It's Dynamic, Not Static

Unlike most other personality testing you might have done in the past, the Enneagram does not simply put you in a box or category, but instead shows you how to develop to become the best version of your personality type.

Each of the 9 types is much more complex than the simple description above might apply, and each type will come across differently depending on where they are on the spectrum of emotional health.

Compatibility?

You are probably wondering at this point whether certain types are more compatible than others. The answer is yes and no...Yes, because some types find it easier to understand and connect with each other, and no, because it depends ultimately on the level of development and self-awareness of each type. A very healthy one, for example, can get along beautifully with a similarly healthy person of any type, whereas an unhealthy two, for example, might find type 9 with its tendency to withdraw unbearably frustrating emotionally.

SO WHAT CAN THE ENNEAGRAM DO TO HELP YOU STRENGTHEN YOUR RELATIONSHIPS?

It Helps People Communicate

By helping we are lucidly conscious of whom and how we are in relationships, what our framework of expectations is, what brings out the best (and the worst) in us, we understand what we need from the other person, and equally what can trigger a negative spiral.

For example, if you're dealing with a heart-centered and aesthetic type Four, you wouldn't approach them initially in an analytical and impersonal way.

It Gives You a Specific Approach and Plan for Maximizing Your Relationships

You can maximize harmony and trust by understanding the enneagram type of your friend, and create a clear plan for allowing the relationship to deliver its potential.

It Helps You Enjoy Your Relationships More

It Helps You Avoid and Resolve Conflict

Each type has a specific pattern in how it deals with conflict, and understanding this pattern allows you to resolve any tension quickly and concentrate on positive solutions instead. Some types deal with conflict by immediately looking for a positive, best-case scenario approach for solutions, whereas others have an emotionally intense response that needs to be understood, and others go into analytical mode. And of course we need all three approaches to resolve conflict successfully.

CHAPTER 5

UNDERSTANDING THE ENNEAGRAM 3 CENTERS - HEART, MIND AND BODY

The Enneagram is a powerful personality typing tool used by coaches and others interested in personal and spiritual growth. In the Enneagram, there are nine different personality types and three centers - or triads - of intelligence, including heart mind and gut. And in each triad there are three different personality types.

In the heart triad lie types 2, 3, and 4. Type 2 is the Giver, 3 is the Performer, and 4 is the Romantic (also sometimes referred to as "Tragic Romantic"). All feel at home in their emotion center or the heart center.

These three types have an emotional thermometer which is going out into the world and testing everyone it bumps into. They come into a room and it's almost like they can probe the people in the room. They're going through questions like, "How are they feeling? How are they reacting to me? What's their emotionally content here?"

Types 2, 3, and 4 - it's all about Image

Types 2, 3, and 4 are the heart triad and are emotion-based. They feel very at home, interacting with the world through emotion, and they are focused on image - on how they are perceived.

They are not just in tune with your responses or emotional content; they're also constantly adjusting themselves because they are concerned with how you are responding to them. They are constantly adjusting themselves to what perceive to be the emotional reactions around them. Each of these three types appears different when they do it.

Types 2, 3, and 4 have an underlying belief that they need to earn value or a sense of worth. Their internal sense of self is largely dependent on what is reflected back to them through others. What the outside world sees in them becomes who they are. This is where their attention is naturally drawn - towards other people's emotional response to them. They are focused on what they do and say - how they project and hold themselves. It's all about appearances.

And this "image thing" goes on and on. It is reflected in the energy they put out, the way they walk, and they way they move. It's even in the jargon they use; for example, you can see Type 3 (Achiever) picking up the jargon in a specific group or social context.

Type 4 is in touch with anything somebody might say that would make them feel less than - or on the outside of - the group. Emotionally they have this huge reactivity to this and response to it.

And Type 2's are paying attention to all the emotions everybody else is having, and what is going on for them. They're asking, "How can I help you out and you're your needs?" It is all tuned all into emotion; that's why it's called the Image Point - they are creating their image based on the emotional way others react to them.

Underneath the surface of 2's, 3's and 4's there is sadness and shame. As they start doing their work, they'll usually bump into underlying signs of shame of who they are, and find they've compensated by trying to be somebody else.

Their thoughts are running along the lines of, "There is something down there that is not right inside me. I can't let people in too close because that internal flaw might be discovered. They can come in, but just not too close. They might discover that thing."

Types 5, 6 and 7 - the Mental Triad

Types 5, 6 and 7 are the head-based types, with an underlining of fear and anxiety.

They live in the world of thinking, cognition and strategizing. The move they've made into the head is about creating safety and control where they won't be "down in the messy emotions" where they are out of control and interacting with "other things" out in the world.

Their thoughts go something like, "Up in the head I can try to understand it. I can think through things. I can create a model for how this world works and then I impose my model onto the world, and I start to believe the model even more then I believe the world."

The Mental types are strategizers - often adept chess players. They understand the world and social situations through the head rather than through the heart (emotions) are body (gut). They are paying attention through the eyes. They are watching and observing to answer questions such as "How are people reacting - in a thinking way - to me?" and "What's going on here?"

For all the head types, there is usually a basic mistrust of the world. For the 5's, people come too close and there is a connection. From this, mistrust develops and they retreat from the world as part of their strategy.

Type 6's are going in and out, but their mistrust is out there in the world. They're thinking, "I can't trust out there." But it's also an internal sense, so they're also thinking, "I can't trust me." Hence there is a lot of dichotomy inside the six's.

The 7 is more of an externalized trust. Their focus of attention is out in the world, sometimes giving their authority away but also not feeling comfortable with that. Then the fears and the anxieties can manifest out in the world, even more then they can inside.

Types 8, 9 and 1 - in the Body and Gut

Types 8, 9 and 9 are the body (or gut)-based types. They feel things through the body. They get energetic hits. When they walk into a room, it's not about the emotion or thinking; rather, they're wondering, "How does this person feel to me - down here in my gut?"

For the body types, there is an underlying anger or resentment that often shows up as judgment. For Type 9, when anger gets repressed, they don't actually let it out. And their needs get repressed.

If you talk to a "young 9" just starting to do their personal work, they'll likely answer, "Anger, what are you talking about? I'm the most mellow, happy-go-lucky, peaceful person I know. I don't know anger.

But as they move deeper into themselves that anger becomes apparent and is often a gateway for them. They will experience a whole new level of self-awareness and expression. For the first time in their lives, they'll understand what their needs are and what they want.

Type 8's tend to externalize the anger. Their energy is much bigger and it comes out. It can overwhelm people and anger can flood into the world. They also tend to not have a sense of other's boundaries. They get their anger out, and like facing others the same way.

Type 1's turn the anger inward. They'll describe an internal critic - a judging voice - that is riding them. It's usually saying something like,

"You have to do it this way. This is what you did wrong. You are stupid. You aren't doing this right. You aren't affective enough. You are not energized enough. You are not (whatever) enough.

This anger is internalized, but often they can also be very judgmental and critical of other folks. There is a defiant internal component for them. Type 1's tend to hold onto the anger in their body.

So those are the three "Centers of Intelligence" - the heart (Types 2, 3 and 4 with an underlying sadness or shame), the head (types 5, 6 and 7 with an underlying fear or anxiety), and the body (types 8, 9 and 1 with underlying anger or judgment).

CHAPTER 6

THE ENNEAGRAM AS A MASTER TOOL FOR TRANSFORMATION

The Enneagram is an ancient tool of uncertain origin, said to be brought in by real genies somehow. Also called the Sufi numbers is like the chess board game and some other things of amazing design that have always been around.

The Enneagram is an outline of the nine basic personality types; it shows the advantages and limitations of every intelligent being born in this planet.

The outline of the nine personality types, with a modern interpretation is as follows.

1. The Perfectionist, The number one is a much disciplined person, wants the best quality at any price. They make pretty good villain

characters in movies because they are very unconcerned with human suffering, they are the perfect inquisitor.

2. The Server, also known as the Helper, or the Saint. They are usually very service oriented people, helping every one. Sometimes they become intrusive manipulators, that want others to do what they want because they feel it is the only right and good way to do it in the Universe. A classic is the beggar that yells at people.

3. The chameleon, also known as climber. This guy is nice and all gifted, but his niceness is just apparent. You can see them changing before your eyes and turning against you as a crisis emerges. Nobody can usually believe that they are fake personalities, because they build a nice smile and an outlook of a good character while in reality they are kind of divorced from their true feelings.

4. The extra sensitive is an artist like personality. Tends to depression and envy of what others have done with their lives. Some suicidal tendencies are possible, because he is aware of his own impulses at the same time that feels guilty about it. For others it may seem as if such a person exaggerates in her emotional concerns about other people's reactions.

5. The paranoid nerd. This guy is very intellectual, but at the same time, he gets distracted. He sees logical connections in everything. He always wants to know the right explanation for the relevant phenomena that occur everywhere. He may get paranoid and build conspiracy theories and cure all remedies. He likes recognition for his brilliant mind and also wants to find a way to fit in the word he sees around as somehow frightening.

6. The devil's advocate. He can be a loyal follower or a bad seditious gossiper enemy. Inside he has a lot of tension that he relieves by finding the worst interpretation possible for others people's behavior, and telling everyone what his twisted mind thinks. He assumes everybody else to be the worst, except the one that he is loyal to. He may look like an unconcerned bastard, but he is a very dutiful hard worker and a masochistic character.

7. The maniac. This guy is peter pan, he never grows up. He is always an immature child. He yells and fights for things and items that he needs so badly that it is even scary. It could be food, videogames, a ticket for the theater, you name it. He is selfish and not too often concerned about sharing the goods evenly.

8. The tyrant dictator. He could also make a great boss or leader. He has a very powerful personality, always grounded in the bottom line. When he is unbalanced he may act as a mafia chief, threatening everybody who doesn't accommodate to his desires. In the positive side he could be a true hero and philanthropist.

9. The nine is the most unavailable person in the planet. A peacemaker kind of alienated unconscious person that lives in a perpetual quiet disconnection. He or she may go with you to a party, and then forget completely that you are there. Sometimes they have awakenings like, Oh my but you have been here all this time!

The Enneagram is in reality a Master tool for transformations, used by group dynamics trainers to create transformational exercises, touching every aspect of the human shadow limitations pool, with the intention to overcome it. It creates the most tremendous breakthroughs in shadow master transformations and it has been a matter for very serious studies.

CHAPTER 7

PERSONAL GROWTH THROUGH THE ENNEAGRAM

Have you ever spent hours on a jigsaw puzzle only to realize that a key piece is missing? Your first response is probably: "It can't be missing. It must be here somewhere." You pick up every available piece in turn. You search under the table and across the floor. You run your fingers over the completed parts of the puzzle, hoping your fingers will see something your eyes have missed.

You can walk away from a jigsaw puzzle that is missing a piece. It is harder to walk away from the hope that your life will come together in a meaningful whole. The Enneagram is a system for thinking about human personality and motivation that helps people understand the patterns in their own lives and the lives of people around them. Many people use the Enneagram to discover the piece they were afraid they were missing.

Based on a combination of ancient wisdom and modern social science, the Enneagram is a model that describes the patterns people typically use to motivate themselves, relate to others and face threats or obstacles. The centre of the system is the recognition that the strategies that work best for us eventually also become the fault lines that leave us vulnerable. We do not always have strengths and weaknesses: sometimes the same quality is both strength and a weakness.

It is one thing to overcome your faults. It is another thing entirely to overcome your strengths. The Enneagram will describe you in terms of what you want most, what you fear most, and what you are likely to do to achieve results you like. It is dynamic in the way that human beings are dynamic; the Enneagram describes how we change when we feel secure or stressed, and how we move between different selves in different contexts. A circle with nine points, the Enneagram describes all of us as part of one whole, a human family in which we are all connected and related.

Much information about the Enneagram is available online and through bookstores. There are many tests that you can take that will start you on the path to understanding your Enneagram type. Within the field of Enneagram studies, tests are only suggestions: they indicate a starting point and not a conclusion. There is no substitute for talking about your patterns with other students of the Enneagram. Just as you have identified yourself through your family and work relationships, you can best identify yourself within the Enneagram tradition by gaining the perspective of other people on the patterns you have been living.

Even a weekend course with a good facilitator will allow you to see more of yourself and to see more in other people. You will begin to identify new pieces of your own personal puzzle and to see the way that other people are building quite different puzzles in their lives. You will have a new perspective to support new quality in your understanding of yourself and your relationship to others.

If you sometimes feel as though you are missing a key piece of your personal puzzle, consider learning more about the Enneagram. You will develop a new sense of how the patterns in your life recur and connect to form a unified whole. You will develop a new understanding of the patterns in other people's behaviors. You will plant the seeds for renewed enthusiasm and satisfaction as you build and sustain relationships.